PHAEDRA

ALSO BY RICHARD WILBUR

The Beautiful Changes and Other Poems
Ceremony and Other Poems
A Bestiary (editor, with Alexander Calder)
Molière's *The Misanthrope* (translator)
Things of This World
Poems 1943–1956
Candide (with Lillian Hellman)
Poe: Complete Poems (editor)
Advice to a Prophet and Other Poems
Molière's *Tartuffe* (translator)
The Poems of Richard Wilbur
Loudmouse (for children)
Shakespeare: Poems (co-editor, with Alfred Harbage)
Walking to Sleep: New Poems and Translations
Molière's *The School for Wives* (translator)
Opposites
The Mind-Reader: New Poems
Responses: Prose Pieces, 1948–1976
Molière's *The Learned Ladies* (translator)
Seven Poems
The Whale & Other Uncollected Translations
Molière: Four Comedies (translator)
Racine's *Andromache* (translator)
New and Collected Poems
More Opposites
Molière's *The School for Husbands* and *Sganarelle* (translator)

JEAN
Racine

PHAEDRA

TRAGEDY IN FIVE ACTS, 1677

TRANSLATED INTO ENGLISH VERSE AND INTRODUCED BY
RICHARD WILBUR

DRAWINGS BY IGOR TULIPANOV

A HARVEST BOOK
HARCOURT BRACE & COMPANY
SAN DIEGO   NEW YORK   LONDON

Library of Congress Cataloging-in-Publication Data
Racine, Jean, 1639–1699.
Phaedra.
Translation of: Phèdre.
I. Phaedra (Greek mythology)—Drama. I. Wilbur,
Richard, 1921– . II. Title. III. Title: Phaedra.
PQ1898.A38   1986   842'.4   86-413
ISBN 0-15-171731-1
ISBN 0-15-675780-X (Harvest: pbk.)

Printed in the United States of America
First Harvest edition 1987
L N P R T S Q O M K

For Charlee

INTRODUCTION

Jean Racine came out with his tenth play, *Phaedra*, in 1677, after which he forsook the theatre except for the requested writing of two religious plays more than a decade later. It is not surely known why a playwright so successful with court and populace all but abandoned his profession at thirty-eight. Some attribute it to his appointment, together with Boileau, to a prestigious task as Louis XIV's royal historiographer. More likely—and for this we have some support from Racine himself—the decision was that of a man who had turned against his early religious training, who had "run with the wolves" as a worldly courtier, lover, and dramatist, and who now felt himself drawn back toward the teachings of his Port Royal mentors—that is, toward the Jansenists. One of the positions of that severe Catholic sect was condemnation of the theatre, and it is not hard to find in the last paragraph of Racine's prose preface to *Phaedra* a gesture of conciliation and an omen of his retirement.

In any case, *Phaedra* embodies a change in Racine's imagination. Though there were certain virtuous characters in his earlier plays, he had always stressed what Oenone in this one calls "our frail estate": the weakness of human beings, their subjection to fatal drives and obsessions, their neglect of moral and social responsibility for the sake of passions which commonly led to unhappy and violent ends. Phaedra, who is the life and center of her play, does not altogether fit into such a vision of the human condition, and is quite unlike, for example, the Hermione of *Andromache*. Far from being the amoral servant of a passion, she is a woman of conscience who perceives and abhors the evil in herself and, with such strength as she has been given, strives against it.

Her heredity, and the wrath of Venus, inflict upon Phaedra a fierce passion for her stepson, Hippolytus—a passion not only adulterous, but also, in the view of the play, incestuous. The guilt-stricken heroine seeks to appease Venus, keeps out of Hippolytus' way, and then in desperation obtains his banishment from Athens to Troezen, to remove temptation and to balk her love by ensuring his enmity. In all of this—though the treatment of Hippolytus involves slander—she is behaving as a virtuous woman hard beset. When her royal husband, Theseus, setting forth on yet another adventure, ironically takes her to Troezen and leaves her under Hippolytus' protection, Phaedra secludes and starves herself, resolved to die without in any way betraying her unabated desire.

These several acts of moral resistance precede the beginning of the play. Within the action of the drama, one may surely view Phaedra's impulse to make Theseus spare his son (Act IV) as a commendable if aborted gesture. She also displays a noble will in her final decision not to die mutely by the sword, but to take her life by the slower means of poison, so that she may have leisure to exonerate Hippolytus and declare her remorse.

Nevertheless, we see her not so much as one who acts, but as one who is remorselessly acted upon. Venus begins by setting Phaedra's veins afire with a passion amounting to possession, and a chain of ensuing events, which seem like malignant interventions, dooms her in her impermissible love not merely to destruction but also to a progressive violation of herself. Under the threat of her nurse Oenone's suicide, and believing that she will shortly die, she makes a first confession of her sinful state. When the absent Theseus is reported to be dead, Oenone urges that Phaedra's love is no longer a crime, and that in any case she must confer with Hippolytus in the political interest of her children. Phaedra's interview with Hippolytus develops into a second confession of her love, this time directed to its horrified object; the confession is, as Racine makes plain, delirious and involuntary. Whereupon Theseus returns alive, and the desperate Phaedra, fearful lest Hippolytus expose her, and misinterpreting his mien, permits Oenone to accuse him to Theseus of an attempt upon the virtue of his queen. Theseus having banished his son, and entreated Neptune to destroy him, the remorseful Phaedra pleads for Hippolytus and is on the verge of confessing her guilt, but is rendered speechless by the news that Hippolytus loves the princess Aricia. Not only does the shock of jealousy put an end to her intercession, but it leads to an hysteria, in which she tells Oenone that "Aricia must die."

Phaedra thus sins by harboring a criminal passion, by avowing it, by conniving at a false accusation which dooms an innocent man, and by desiring the death of an innocent woman. Yet she is at all times an object of sympathy. This is, once more, because she sees her guilt clearly and condemns it, because she struggles against her illicit feelings, and because—in this play which is really a delayed suicide —she wishes to perish rather than pollute the world with her "foulness." We sympathize also because the outrageous events of the plot—her being taken to Troezen, the false report of Theseus' death, his return, his revelation of Hippolytus' love for another—are too much for her, reducing her to distraction and a dependence on Oenone's counsels. First and last, we must compassionate Phaedra because her basic sin of guilty infatuation has been divinely thrust upon her; because, in Louis Auchincloss' plain words, she "is a lost soul through no fault of her own."

The great scenes of the drama are all Phaedra's, and it has been noted that the interest of the other main characters, varied as they are, lies to some extent in their being versions of her. If Phaedra is a good woman who yearns for innocence and is afflicted with lust, Theseus is a heroic cleanser of the world, a slayer of monsters and brigands, whose splendid history has been marred by amorous abductions and betrayals. It is this amorousness, his chief weakness, which prevents him from understanding his chaste son and disposes him to believe Oenone's slander. The other faults which contribute to his tragic blunder are a precipitate violence and an obsession with his honor. Hippolytus, Theseus' son by an Amazonian queen, is a proud, valorous, and idealistic young man, austerely resistant to love, who nonetheless loses his heart to Aricia. This Racine describes as a "frailty," since King Theseus has, for political reasons, forbidden Aricia to marry. It is one measure of Hippolytus' filial devotion that, during a good portion of the play, he regards his love as culpable. Racine's construction of the first two acts has been praised by Michel Autrand for its emphatic paralleling of the behaviors of Phaedra and Hippolytus: each character reveals to a confidant a "forbidden" love; each approaches the beloved, prompted by Theseus' reported death, to discuss who now shall rule; each proceeds to make a helpless avowal of passion. This apposition stresses Venus' irresistible power to induce love, of one kind or another, in an unwilling heart; and Aricia, of course, gives supporting evidence. She, like Hippolytus, has been "a lifelong enemy of love," and she comes to love the pure, untamed Hippolytus for having been the same. Whatever their natures, in short, the characters truly instrumental in Phaedra's story—even Oenone, whose sole motive is blind fidelity to her mistress—are subjected by Venus and, like the heroine, brought to grief through the consequences of some species of love.

Though the one day's drama of *Phaedra* takes place within or before a palace in Troezen, its dialogue makes it extraordinarily expansive in space and time. Of Troezen itself we gain, on the whole, only disjunct glimpses. A stage direction, for instance, tells us of a chair in the sunlight. We are several times told that there are woods in which one might hunt or be concealed. Phaedra lets it drop that the palace architecture is vaulted, and gives us a two-line glimpse of Hippolytus' ships in the harbor, their prows pointed toward Athens. There is ship talk from Hippolytus and Theramenes as well. Oenone begins to describe the town's tumultuous response to Theseus' landing and approach, but is interrupted. The most sustained and detailed picture of Troezen lies just beyond its gates, where we see an ancient burial site, the temple where Aricia and Hippolytus plan in vain to marry, and the road, shore, and brambled rocks which figure in Theramenes' account of Hippolytus' death. Troezen is, in any concrete sense, a fragmentary place, and we experience it mainly as the locus of intense psychological actions and reactions. And yet, in the play's second speech, we hear of Theramenes' vast search for Theseus, which takes him from Epirus to that far sea, near Asia Minor, where Icarus was drowned; we are reminded of Theseus' long and far-flung exploits, extending in fable even to Hades; and through repeated reference we recall the wide-ranging Hercules. A whole Mediterranean world, full of names like Scythia and Mycenae, surrounds Troezen, and Theseus speaks even of a realm "beyond Alcides' pillars." As for history, the play is haunted by a consciousness of the Cretan saga, and the tale of Athens is carried back to Aegeus, Pallas, Erectheus. It belongs to the largeness of the play that Phaedra ends her life with a poison once brought to Athens by the Colchian Medea.

The dimensions of the play are also enlarged by the fact that its persons, though mortal, may claim descent or special favor from the Gods. Aricia's line goes back to Earth. On her mother's side, Phaedra is the granddaughter of the Sun, and since her father, Minos, was sired by the highest of the Gods, she may say that she and her children are of "the blood of Jove." Theseus is protected by Neptune, who also taught Hippolytus the art of training horses. What is to be made of this presence of the divine—so

much greater than in his earlier works—in Racine's last
"secular" tragedy? One scholar argues interestingly that,
given the playwright's conceptions of the principals and
his plans for their dramatic development, Hippolytus can
die only by divine agency, and that for such a death to be
credible, it must be prepared for by an atmosphere constantly infused with the supernatural, the fabulous, the
monstrous. I cannot find that answer sufficient, practical
though it sounds in terms of stagecraft. This is because, as
I read *Phaedra,* not all of the Gods are machinery or décor;
though remote, some of them are terribly real, and
shadow forth that religious vision to which Racine was
returning.

Consider Venus. Since the criminal passion central to the
play is erotic in nature, she is often said to have caused it,
but we are never for a moment told why. One available
answer, given in part by Demodocus in the eighth book of
the *Odyssey,* was that because the Sun had revealed to Vul-
can the guilty loves of Venus and Mars, Venus thereafter
persecuted the descendants of the Sun. But Racine nowhere
alludes to this motive or any other, and in his preface and
elsewhere repeatedly treats Phaedra's involuntary crime
more generally as "a punishment of the Gods." "Heaven,"
says Phaedra in her dying speech, "lit a fatal blaze within
my breast." Since no motive for Venus is stated, and since
Phaedra is frequently seen as arbitrarily afflicted by all of
supernature, one discerns in the background of the play
that harsh version of Christianity called Jansenism, in
which the human soul is too corrupt to seek salvation ac-
tively, and an inscrutable God damns or saves as it pleases
Him. In such a perspective, Venus' persecution is God's
chastisement of the nonelect, the Sun is His all-seeing eye,
and the shade of Minos is the executor of His judgment.
And now that we are on Christian ground, we may sense in
the hereditary sufferings of Phaedra's line the Biblical idea
(Exodus 20:5) that the Lord visits the iniquity of the fathers

upon the children unto the third and fourth generation.

Such guilt and inner conflict as Racine's heroine feels are not to be found in the characters of his classical models, or of his own earlier plays. Phaedra is, as a number of critics have said, "a Greek woman with a Christian conscience." The Jansenist theologian Antoine Arnauld is said to have called her "one of the just to whom grace was not vouchsafed." Though she speaks of preserving her honor or good name, her true and hopeless hunger is for innocence, for a state of soul called "purity," which both she and Hippolytus associate with the *jour*, the clean light of day. And "purity," indeed, is the last word spoken by her dying lips. Her great speech in Act IV, Scene 6, in which she feels her sins exposed to the gaze of all her immortal kin in Earth and Sky and Hades, represents the ultimate expansion of the play's scope, an expansion rendered all the greater by its Christian overtones.

This translation preserves the rhymed verse of the original, though the alexandrine is replaced by our corresponding English meter, the pentameter. It is no triumph that my translation, like the original, has exactly 1,654 lines, but it is an indication that the thought and tone of Racine's line, even at its most compressed, can readily pass into our traditional dramatic measure. Where I have used slightly more enjambment than Racine, it is mostly because English meters are more emphatic and less flowing than the French; too long a sequence of end-stopped English lines, especially if rhymed, can sound like the stacking of planks in a lumberyard. And as for sound, I must say something about the celebrated sonority of Racine. Since French does not sound or move like English, a translator who sought to duplicate the "music" of certain famous lines in *Phaedra* would in the first place fail, and, second, would doubtless slight the matter and tone, which are primary in all writing. What one must do, I think, is to try throughout for equivalent effects of significant sound and pacing in the key of English, and remember always that one is seeking to be worthy of a magnificent ear.

In her crucial exchange with Hippolytus in Act II, Scene 5, Phaedra abruptly ceases to address him as *vous*, and employs the *tu* instead. What is to be done about that? "Thou" is largely obsolete in English as affectionate address, and would violate the diction of the translation, which aims to be as undated as possible; the insertion of an endearment would falsify the mood of the scene; one must be content with the fact that Phaedra's change of pronoun coincides with her sudden, explicit, and translatable admission that she is "insane with love" for Hippolytus. The question of *tu* arises also when the Gods are addressed, as Neptune by Theseus or Venus by Phaedra. Though in rendering *Andromache* several years ago, I had Orestes upbraid the Gods as "Thou," it seemed more suitable in the present cases, given the tenor of the appeals, to employ the "You," while preserving the tone of entreaty. Readers and hearers will have to decide whether I was right or not.

Another challenge to the translator comes in Act V, where Theramenes' account of Hippolytus' death and Aricia's grief shifts several times between a past tense and the historical present. Such transitions are common and conventional in the verse of Dryden or Pope, but may seem less "natural" in a contemporary translation. Still, *Phaedra* being a play, I have for theatrical reasons taken the risk of following Racine's handling of this exceptionally long specimen of the "messenger's speech." Theramenes is speaking to Theseus, but he is also reliving and reseeing horrors which have just occurred. A good actor would, I think, know how to modulate into the present tense, so as to give the events described a greater immediacy. Let me add, incidentally, that such a good actor would not pronounce the name Aricia as if it rhymed with "militia."

Elsewhere I have said at length why one or another classic French drama ought to be rendered both in meter and

[*Introduction*]

in rhyme. Many of those former arguments would be perti-
nent here, but I shall not repeat them. Consider only this
—the closing lines of that soliloquy (Act IV, Scene 5) in
which Phaedra, frenzied with jealousy, justifies her failure
to intercede successfully for Hippolytus, saying of him
what her saner self knows to be untrue:

> And yet another's made his pride surrender;
> Another's made his cruel eyes grow tender.
> Perhaps his heart is easy to ensnare.
> It's me, alone of women, he cannot bear!
> Shall I defend a man by whom I'm spurned?

In such a passage, the irrational leaps of the self-deceiving
mind are sharply emphasized by the contrasting coherence
of the form, which embodies an ideal of high and orderly
consciousness.

I must thank the many commentators whose writings
have strengthened my purchase on *Phaedra*. I also acknowl-
edge a debt, for a number of words and phrases, to previous
translations in blank verse. My thanks to those who encour-
aged me to do the translation; also to the Witter Bynner
Foundation for Poetry; to the Academy of American Poets;
to Smith College; to the Camargo Foundation, at which
most of the job was done; and to certain Camargo scholars
—Rudolph Binion, Patrice Higgonet, Jesse Dickson, Mi-
chael Pretina—who helped me with troublesome passages.
James Merrill has my particular gratitude for criticizing the
first act and for reshaping a crucial couplet. The kind
suggestions of Alfred Corn were of great value to me, as
were those of Sonja and William Jay Smith. And my wife
could not possibly be thanked enough for her patient con-
sideration of every word.

Richard Wilbur

Cummington, Massachusetts
1985

PHAEDRA

CHARACTERS

THESEUS, son of Aegeus, King of Athens

PHAEDRA, wife of Theseus, daughter of Minos and Pasiphaë

HIPPOLYTUS, son of Theseus and Antiope, Queen of the
Amazons

ARICIA, princess of the blood royal of Athens

THERAMENES, Hippolytus' tutor

OENONE, Phaedra's nurse and confidante

ISMENE, Aricia's confidante

PANOPE, lady-in-waiting to Phaedra

GUARDS

The action takes place within and without a palace at
Troezen, a town in the Peloponnesus.

RACINE'S PREFACE TO
PHAEDRA (1677)

Here is another tragedy whose subject is borrowed from Euripides. Though I have taken a somewhat different path from that author's, as regards the conduct of the action, I have not failed to enrich my play with everything which seemed to me most striking in his. Even if I owed him no more than the mere idea of the figure of Phaedra, I could say that I owe to him what is perhaps the most compelling character I have put upon the stage. I am not at all surprised that this role had so happy a reception in Euripides' day, and that it should also have been so successful in our own, since it possesses all of those qualities which Aristotle required in a hero of tragedy, and which are capable of exciting pity and terror. Phaedra is, in fact, neither wholly guilty nor wholly innocent. She is ensnared, through her destiny and through the wrath of the Gods, in an illegitimate passion by which she is the very first to be horrified. She does everything she can to overcome it. She had rather let herself die than make it known to anyone. And when she is forced to reveal it, she speaks of it with a shame which makes it quite clear that her crime is a divine punishment rather than the product of her own will.

I have further taken care to make her somewhat less odious than she is in the tragedies of the Ancients, where she herself resolves to accuse Hippolytus. I felt that the calumny was rather too base and foul to be put into the mouth of a princess whose sentiments were otherwise so noble and so virtuous. Such baseness seemed to me more suitable to a nurse, who might be expected to have more servile inclinations—but who nevertheless makes the false accusation only to save the life and honor of her mistress. Phaedra agrees to it only because she is in such agitation as

3

to be unbalanced in mind, and she returns but a moment later with the intention of clearing the innocent and declaring the truth.

The blameless Hippolytus is accused, in Euripides and in Seneca, with having in fact violated his stepmother: *vim corpus tulit.* But in this play he is accused only of having had the intention to do so. I wished to spare Theseus a degree of violent feeling which might have made him less sympathetic to the audience.

As for the figure of Hippolytus, I had noticed that Euripides was reproached among the Ancients for having depicted him as a philosopher free of all imperfections: the result of which was that the death of the young prince caused far more indignation than pity. I thought it best to give him some frailty which would render him slightly guilty toward his father, without however detracting in any way from that greatness of soul which leads him to spare Phaedra's honor, and to suffer ill-treatment without accusing her. I call it a frailty that he feels, despite himself, a passion for Aricia, who is the daughter and sister of his father's mortal enemies.

This Aricia is not a figure of my own invention. Virgil says that Hippolytus married her, and had a son by her, after Aesculapius had restored him to life. And I have read also in certain authors that Hippolytus wedded and took to Italy a high-born young Athenian woman, who was called Aricia, and who gave her name to a small Italian town.

I mention these authorities because I have made a very scrupulous effort to follow the classic fable. I have likewise followed the history of Theseus, as we have it in Plutarch.

In that historian I found that what had given rise to the belief in Theseus' descent into Hades to abduct Proserpina was in fact a journey which the prince had made into Epirus, near the source of the Acheron, where a king, whose wife Pirithoüs wished to carry off, held Theseus prisoner, having first put Pirithoüs to death. Accordingly I have sought to retain the credibility of history, without sacrificing any of the embellishments of fable, which is such a rich mine of poetry. The rumor of Theseus' death, based on the fabulous journey to Hades, is the occasion of Phaedra's declaration of love, which becomes a principal cause of her undoing, and which she would never have dared make had she believed her husband to be alive.

For the rest, I do not yet dare assert that this play is in fact the best of my tragedies. I leave it to my readers, and to time, to decide as to its true worth. What I can assert is that no play of mine so celebrates virtue as this one does. The least faults are here severely punished. The mere thought of crime is seen with as much horror as the crime itself. Weaknesses begot by love are treated here as real weaknesses; the passions are here represented only to show all the disorder which they bring about; and vice is everywhere painted in colors which make one know and hate its deformity. To do thus is the proper end which every man who writes for the public should propose to himself; and this is what, above all, the earliest tragic poets had in view. Their theatre was a school in which virtue was taught no less well than in the schools of the philosophers. Therefore Aristotle consented to establish rules for the dramatic poem; and Socrates, the wisest of the philosophers, deigned to have a hand in the writing of Euripides' tragedies. It would be a highly desirable thing if our current writings were as sound, and as full of wholesome instruction, as the works of those poets. Were that so, it might be a means of reconciling to tragedy many persons, celebrated for their piety and good doctrine, who have of late condemned it, and who would doubtless judge it more favorably if our playwrights were as concerned to edify as to divert their audiences, thus fulfilling the true purpose of tragedy.

ACT I

SCENE ONE

HIPPOLYTUS, THERAMENES

HIPPOLYTUS

No, dear Theramenes, I've too long delayed
In pleasant Troezen; my decision's made.
I'm off; in my anxiety, I commence
To tax myself with shameful indolence.
My father has been gone six months and more,
And yet I do not know what distant shore
Now hides him, or what trials he now may bear.

THERAMENES

You'll go in search of him, my lord? But where?
Already, to appease your fears, I've plied
The seas which lie on Corinth's either side;
I've asked for Theseus among tribes who dwell
Where Acheron goes plunging into Hell;
Elis I've searched and, from Taenarus bound,
Reached even that sea where Icarus was drowned.
In what fresh hope, in what unthought-of places,
Do you set out to find your father's traces?
Who knows, indeed, if he wants the truth about
His long, mysterious absence to come out,
And whether, while we tremble for him, he's
Not fondling some new conquest at his ease
And planning to deceive her like the rest? . . .

9

HIPPOLYTUS

Enough, Theramenes. In King Theseus' breast,
The foolish fires of youth have ceased to burn;
No tawdry dalliance hinders his return.
Phaedra need fear no rivals now; the King
Long since, for her sake, ceased philandering,
I go then, out of duty—and as a way
To flee a place in which I dare not stay.

THERAMENES

Since when, my lord, have you begun to fear
This peaceful place your childhood held so dear,
And which I've often known you to prefer
To Athens' court, with all its pomp and stir?
What danger or affliction drives you hence?

HIPPOLYTUS

Those happy times are gone. All's altered since
The Gods dispatched to us across the sea
The child of Minos and Pasiphaë.

THERAMENES

Ah. Then it's Phaedra's presence in this place
That weighs on you. She'd hardly seen your face
When, as the King's new consort, she required
Your banishment, and got what she desired.
But now her hatred for you, once so great,
Has vanished, or has cooled, at any rate.
And why, my lord, should you feel threatened by
A dying woman who desires to die?
Sick unto death—with what, she will not say,

Weary of life and of the light of day,
Could Phaedra plot to do you any harm?

HIPPOLYTUS

Her vain hostility gives me no alarm.
It is, I own, another enemy,
The young Aricia, from whom I flee,
Last of a line which sought to overthrow
Our house.

THERAMENES

What! Will you also be her foe?
That gentle maiden, though of Pallas' line,
Had no part in her brothers' base design.
If she is guiltless, why should you hate her, Sir?

HIPPOLYTUS

I would not flee her if I hated her.

THERAMENES

Dare I surmise, then, why you're leaving us?
Are you no longer that Hippolytus
Who spurned love's dictates and refused with scorn
The yoke which Theseus has so often borne?
Has Venus, long offended by your pride,
Contrived to see her Theseus justified
By making you confess her power divine
And bow, like other men, before her shrine?
Are you in love, Sir?

HIPPOLYTUS

What do you mean, dear man—
You who have known me since my life began?
How can you wish that my austere and proud
Persuasions be so basely disavowed?
I sucked that pride which seems so strange to you
From an Amazonian mother, and when I grew
To riper years, and knew myself, I thought
My given nature to be nobly wrought.
You then, devoted friend, instructed me
In all my father's brilliant history,
And you recall how glowingly I heard
His exploits, how I hung on every word
As you portrayed a sire whose deeds appease
Men's longing for another Hercules—
Those monsters slain, those brigands all undone,
Procrustes, Sciron, Sinis, Cercyon,—
The Epidaurian giant's scattered bones,
The Minotaur's foul blood on Cretan stones!
But when you told me of less glorious feats,
His far-flung chain of amorous deceits,
Helen of Sparta kidnapped as a maid;
Sad Periboea in Salamis betrayed;
Others, whose very names escape him now,
Too-trusting hearts, deceived by sigh and vow;
Wronged Ariadne, telling the rocks her moan,
Phaedra abducted, though to grace a throne,—
You know how, loathing stories of that sort,
I begged you oftentimes to cut them short,
And wished posterity might never hear
The worser half of Theseus' great career.
Shall I, in my turn, be subjected so
To passion, by the Gods be brought so low—
The more disgraced because I cannot claim
Such honors as redeem King Theseus' name,

And have not, by the blood of monsters, won
The right to trespass as my sire has done?
And even if my pride laid down its arms,
Could I surrender to Aricia's charms?
Would not my wayward passions heed the ban
Forbidding her to me, or any man?
The King's no friend to her, and has decreed
That she not keep alive her brothers' seed;
Fearing some new shoot from their guilty stem,
He wants her death to be the end of them;
For her, the nuptial torch shall never blaze;
He's doomed her to be single all her days.
Shall I take up her cause then, brave his rage,
Set a rebellious pattern for the age,
Commit my youth to love's delirium . . . ?

THERAMENES

Ah, Sir, if love's appointed hour has come,
It's vain to reason; Heaven will not hear.
What Theseus bans, he makes you hold more dear.
His hate for her but stirs your flames the more,
And lends new grace to her whom you adore.
Why fear, my lord, a love that's true and chaste?
Of what's so sweet, will you not dare to taste?
Shall timid scruples make your blood congeal?
What Hercules once felt, may you not feel?
What hearts has Venus' power failed to sway?
Where would you be, who strive with her today,
If fierce Antiope had not grown tame
And loved King Theseus with a virtuous flame?
But come, my lord, why posture and debate?
Admit that you have changed, and that of late
You're seen less often, in your lonely pride,
Racing your chariot by the oceanside,
Or deftly using Neptune's art to train

13

Some charger to obey the curb and rein.
The woods less often echo to our cries.
A secret fire burns in your heavy eyes.
No question of it: you're sick with love, you feel
A wasting passion which you would conceal.
Has fair Aricia wakened your desire?

HIPPOLYTUS

I'm off, Theramenes, to find my sire.

THERAMENES

Will you not see the Queen before you go,
My lord?

HIPPOLYTUS

I mean to. You may tell her so.
Duty requires it of me. Ah, but here's
Her dear Oenone; what new grief prompts her tears?

Who is Hippo in love with?

SCENE TWO

HIPPOLYTUS, OENONE, THERAMENES

OENONE

Alas, my lord, what grief could equal mine?
The Queen has gone into a swift decline.
I nurse her, tend her day and night, but she
Is dying of some nameless malady.
Disorder rules within her heart and head.
A restless pain has dragged her from her bed;
She longs to see the light; but in her keen
Distress she is unwilling to be seen. . . .
She's coming.

HIPPOLYTUS

       I understand, and I shall go.
My hated face would but increase her woe.

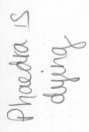

Phaedra is dying

SCENE THREE

PHAEDRA

Let's go no farther; stay, Oenone dear.
I'm faint; my strength abandons me, I fear.
My eyes are blinded by the glare of day,
And now I feel my trembling knees give way.
Alas!

(She sits.)

OENONE

O Gods, abate our misery!

PHAEDRA

These veils, these baubles, how they burden me!
What meddling hand has twined my hair, and made
Upon my brow so intricate a braid?
All things oppress me, vex me, do me ill.

OENONE

Her wishes war against each other still.
'Twas you who, full of self-reproach, just now

16

Insisted that our hands adorn your brow;
You who called back your strength so that you might
Come forth again and once more see the light.
Yet, seeing it, you all but turn and flee,
Hating the light which you came forth to see.

PHAEDRA

Founder of our sad race, bright god of fire,
You whom my mother dared to boast her sire,
Who blush perhaps to see my wretched case,
For the last time, O Sun, I see your face.

OENONE

Can't you shake off that morbid wish? Must I
Forever hear you laying plans to die?
What is this pact with death which you have made?

PHAEDRA

Oh, to be sitting in the woods' deep shade!
When shall I witness, through a golden wrack
Of dust, a chariot flying down the track?

OENONE

What, Madam?

PHAEDRA

　　　　Where am I? Madness! What did I say?
Where have I let my hankering senses stray?

The Gods have robbed me of my wits. A rush
Of shame, Oenone, causes me to blush.
I make my guilty torments all too plain.
My eyes, despite me, fill with tears of pain.

OENONE

If you must blush, then blush for your perverse
Silence, which only makes your sickness worse.
Spurning our care, and deaf to all we say—
Is it your cruel design to die this way?
What madness dooms your life in middle course?
What spell, what poison has dried up its source?
Three times the night has overrun the skies
Since sleep last visited your hollow eyes,
And thrice the day has made dim night retreat
Since you, though starving, have refused to eat.
What frightful evil does your heart intend?
What right have you to plot your own life's end?
You thereby wrong the Gods who authored you;
Betray the spouse to whom your faith is due;
Betray your children by the selfsame stroke,
And thrust their necks beneath a heavy yoke.
Yes, on the day their mother's life is done,
Proud hopes will stir in someone else's son—
Your foe, the foe of all your lineage, whom
An Amazon once carried in her womb:
Hippolytus . . .

PHAEDRA

Gods!

OENONE

My words strike home at last.

PHAEDRA

Oh, wretched woman, what was that name which passed
Your lips?

OENONE

        Ah, now you're roused to anger. Good.
That name has made you shudder, as it should.
Live, then. Let love and duty fire your spirit.
Live, lest a Scythian's son should disinherit
Your children, lest he crush the noblest fruit
Of Greece and of the Gods beneath his boot.
But lose no time; each moment now could cost
Your life; retrieve the strength that you have lost,
While still your feeble fires, which sink so low,
Smoulder and may be fanned into a glow.

PHAEDRA

Alas, my guilty flame has burnt too long.

OENONE

Come, what remorse can flay you so? What wrong
Can you have done to be so crushed with guilt?
There is no innocent blood your hands have spilt.

PHAEDRA

My hands, thank Heaven, are guiltless, as you say.
Gods! That my heart were innocent as they!

OENONE

What fearful notion can your thoughts have bred,
So that your heart still shrinks from it in dread?

[*Act One* · *Scene Three*]

PHAEDRA

I've said enough, Oenone. Spare me the rest
I die, to keep that horror unconfessed.

OENONE

Then die, and keep your heartless silence, do.
But someone else must close your eyes for you
Although your flickering life has all but fled,
I shall go down before you to the dead.
There are a thousand roads that travel there;
I'll choose the shortest, in my just despair.
O cruel mistress! When have I failed or grieved you?
Remember: at your birth, these arms received you.
For you I left my country, children, kin:
Is this the prize my faithfulness should win?

PHAEDRA

What can you gain by this? Why rant and scold?
You'd shake with terror if the truth were told.

OENONE

Great Gods! What words could match the terror I
Must daily suffer as I watch you die?

PHAEDRA

When you have learnt my crime, my fate, my shame,
I'll die no less, but with a guiltier name.

[*Act One* · *Scene Three*]

OENONE

My lady, by the tears which stain my face,
And by your trembling knees which I embrace,
Enlighten me; deliver me from doubt.

PHAEDRA

You've asked it. Rise.

OENONE

                I'm listening. Come, speak out.

PHAEDRA

O Gods! What shall I say to her? Where shall I start?

OENONE

Speak, speak. Your hesitations wound my heart.

PHAEDRA

Alas, how Venus hates us! As Love's thrall,
Into what vileness did my mother fall!

OENONE

Dear Queen, forget it; to the end of time
Let silence shroud the memory of that crime.

PHAEDRA

O sister Ariadne! Through love, once more,
You died abandoned on a barren shore!

OENONE

Madam, what's this? What anguish makes you trace
So bitterly the tale of all your race?

PHAEDRA

And now, since Venus wills it, I must pine
And die, the last of our accursèd line.

OENONE

You are in love?

PHAEDRA

I feel love's raging thirst.

OENONE

For whom?

PHAEDRA

Of all dire things, now hear the worst.
I love . . . From that dread name I shrink, undone;
I love . . .

OENONE

Whom?

22

PHAEDRA

Think of a Scythian woman's son,
A prince I long ill-used and heaped with blame.

OENONE

Hippolytus? Gods!

PHAEDRA

'Twas you who spoke his name.

OENONE

Just Heaven! All my blood begins to freeze.
O crime, despair, most curst of families!
Why did we voyage to this ill-starred land
And set our feet upon its treacherous strand?

PHAEDRA

My ills began far earlier. Scarcely had I
Pledged with Aegeus' son our marriage-tie,
Secure in that sweet joy a bride should know,
When I, in Athens, met my haughty foe.
I stared, I blushed, I paled, beholding him;
A sudden turmoil set my mind aswim;
My eyes no longer saw, my lips were dumb;
My body burned, and yet was cold and numb.
I knew myself possessed by Venus, whose
Fierce flames torment the quarry she pursues.
I thought to appease her then by constant prayer,
And built for her a temple, decked with care.
I made continual sacrifice, and sought
In entrails for a spirit less distraught—

But what could cure a lovesick soul like mine?
In vain my hands burnt incense at her shrine:
Though I invoked the Goddess' name, 'twas he
I worshiped; I saw his image constantly,
And even as I fed the altar's flame
Made offering to a god I dared not name.
I shunned him; but—O horror and disgrace!—
My eyes beheld him in his father's face.
At last I knew that I must act, must urge
Myself, despite myself, to be his scourge.
To rid me of the foe I loved, I feigned
A harsh stepmother's malice, and obtained
By ceaseless cries my wish that he be sent
From home and father into banishment.
I breathed once more, Oenone; once he was gone,
My blameless days could flow more smoothly on.
I hid my grief, was faithful to my spouse,
And reared the offspring of our luckless vows.
Ah, mocking Fate! What use was all my care?
Brought by my spouse himself to Troezen, there
I yet again beheld my exiled foe:
My unhealed wound began once more to flow.
Love hides no longer in these veins, at bay:
Great Venus fastens on her helpless prey.
I look with horror on my crime; I hate
My life; my passion I abominate.
I hoped by death to keep my honor bright,
And hide so dark a flame from day's pure light:
Yet, yielding to your tearful argument,
I've told you all; of that I'll not repent
Provided you do not, as death draws near,
Pour more unjust reproaches in my ear,
Or seek once more in vain to fan a fire
Which flickers and is ready to expire.

SCENE FOUR

PANOPE

Madam, there's grievous news which I'd withhold
If I were able; but it must be told.
Death's claimed your lord, who feared no other foe—
Of which great loss you are the last to know.

OENONE

You tell us, Panope . . . ?

PANOPE

                That the Queen in vain
Prays for her Theseus to return again;
That mariners have come to port, from whom
Hippolytus has learned his father's doom.

PHAEDRA

Gods!

PANOPE

Who'll succeed him, Athens can't agree.
The Prince your son commands much loyalty,

25

My lady; yet, despite their country's laws,
Some make the alien woman's son their cause;
Some plot, they say, to put in Theseus' place
Aricia, the last of Pallas' race.
Of both these threats I thought that you should know.
Hippolytus has rigged his ship to go,

And if, in Athens' ferment, he appeared,
The fickle mob might back him, it is feared.

OENONE

Enough. The Queen has heard you. She'll give thought
To these momentous tidings you have brought.

Theseus is
dead

SCENE FIVE

PHAEDRA, OENONE

OENONE

Mistress, I'd ceased to urge you not to die;
I thought to follow you to the grave, since my
Dissuasions had no longer any force:
But this dark news prescribes a change of course.
Your destiny now wears a different face:
The King is dead, and you must take his place.
He leaves a son who needs your sheltering wing—
A slave without you; if you live, a king.
Who else will soothe his orphan sorrows, pray?
If you are dead, who'll wipe his tears away?
His innocent cries, borne up to Heaven, will make
The Gods, his forebears, curse you for his sake.
Live, then: there's nothing now you're guilty of.
Your love's become like any other love.
With Theseus' death, those bonds exist no more
Which made your passion something to abhor.
Hippolytus need no longer cause you fear;
Seeing him now, your conscience can be clear.
Perhaps, convinced that you're his bitter foe,
He means to lead the rebels. Make him know
His error; win him over; stay his hand.
He's king, by right, of Troezen's pleasant land;
But as for bright Minerva's citadel,
It is your son's by law, as he knows well.

You should, indeed, join forces, you and he:
Aricia is your common enemy.

PHAEDRA

So be it. By your advice I shall be led;
I'll live, if I can come back from the dead,
And if my mother-love still has the power
To rouse my weakened spirits in this hour.

Phaedra will ≠ talk to Hypp

Aricia is a threat

ACT II

SCENE ONE

ARICIA, ISMENE

ARICIA

Hippolytus asks to see me? Can this be?
He seeks me out to take his leave of me?
There's no mistake, Ismene?

ISMENE

Indeed, there's not.
This shows how Theseus' death has changed your lot.
Expect now to receive from every side
The homage which, through him, you've been denied.
At last, Aricia rules her destiny;
Soon, at her feet, all Greece shall bend the knee.

ARICIA

This is no doubtful rumor, then? I've shed
The bonds of slavery? My oppressor's dead?

ISMENE

The Gods relent, my lady. It is so.
Theseus has joined your brothers' shades below.

imagining

31

ARICIA

And by what mishap did he come to grief?

ISMENE

The tales are many, and they strain belief.
Some say that he, abducting from her home
A new beloved, was swallowed by the foam.
It's even thought, as many tongues now tell,
That, faring with Pirithoüs down to Hell,
He walked alive amid the dusky ranks
Of souls, and saw Cocytus' dismal banks,
But found himself a prisoner in that stern
Domain from which no mortal can return.

ARICI*

Shall I believe that, while he still draws breath,
A man can penetrate the realms of death?
What spell could lure him to that fearsome tract?

ISMENE

Theseus is dead. You, only, doubt the fact.
All Athens grieves; the news was scarcely known
When Troezen raised Hippolytus to its throne.
Here in this palace, trembling for her son,
Phaedra confers on what must now be done.

ARICIA

You think Hippolytus will be more kind
Than Theseus was to me, that he'll unbind
My chains, and show me pity?

ISMENE

Madam, I do.

ARICIA

Isn't the man's cold nature known to you?
What makes you think that, scorning women, he
Will yet show pity and respect to me?
He long has shunned us, and as you well know
Haunts just those places where we do not go.

ISMENE

He's called, I know, the most austere of men,
But I have seen him in your presence, when,
Intrigued by his repute, I thought to observe
His celebrated pride and cold reserve.
His manner contradicted all I'd heard:
At your first glance, I saw him flushed and stirred.
His eyes, already full of languor, tried
To leave your face, but could not turn aside.
He has, though love's a thing he may despise,
If not a lover's tongue, a lover's eyes.

ARICIA

Ismene, how your words delight my ear!
Even if baseless, they are sweet to hear.
O you who know me, can you believe of me,
Sad plaything of a ruthless destiny,
Forever fed on tears and bitterness,
That love could touch me, and its dear distress?
Last offspring of that king whom Earth once bore,
I only have escaped the rage of war.

I lost six brothers, young and fresh as May,
In whom the hopes of our great lineage lay:
The sharp sword reaped them all; Earth, soaked and red,
Drank sadly what Erectheus' heirs had shed.
You know that, since their death, a harsh decree
Forbids all Greeks to pay their court to me,
Lest, through my progeny, I should revive
My brothers' ashes, and keep their cause alive.
But you know too with what disdain I bore
The ban of our suspicious conqueror.
You know how I, a lifelong enemy
Of love, gave thanks for Theseus' tyranny,
Since he forbade what I was glad to shun.
But then . . . but then I had not seen his son.
Not that my eyes alone, charmed by his grace,
Have made me love him for his form or face,
Mere natural gifts for which he seems to care
But little, or of which he's unaware.
I find in him far nobler gifts than these—
His father's strengths, without his frailties.
I love, I own, a heart that's never bowed
Beneath Love's yoke, but stayed aloof and proud.
Small glory Phaedra gained from Theseus' sighs!
More proud than she, I spurn the easy prize
Of love-words said a thousand times before,
And of a heart that's like an open door.
Ah, but to move a heart that's firm as stone,
To teach it pangs which it has never known,
To bind my baffled captive in a chain
Against whose sweet constraint he strives in vain:
There's what excites me in Hippolytus; he's
A harder conquest than was Hercules,
Whose heart, so often vanquished and inflamed,
Less honored those by whom he had been tamed.
But, dear Ismene, how rashly I have talked!
My hopes may all too easily be balked,

34

And I may humbly grieve in future days
Because of that same pride which now I praise.
What! Can Hippolytus love? By some blest turn
Of fortune can it be . . . ?

ISMENE

You'll shortly learn;
He's coming.

SCENE TWO

HIPPOLYTUS, ARICIA, ISMENE

HIPPOLYTUS

Madam, I felt, ere leaving here,
That I should make your altered fortunes clear.
My sire is dead. My fears divined, alas,
By his long absence, what had come to pass.
Death only, ending all his feats and frays,
Could hide him from the world so many days.
The Gods have yielded to destroying Fate
Hercules' heir and friend and battle-mate.
Although you hated him, I trust that you
Do not begrudge such praise as was his due.
One thought, however, soothes my mortal grief:
I now may offer you a just relief,
Revoking the most cruel of decrees.
Your heart, your hand, bestow them as you please;
For here in Troezen, where I now shall reign,
Which was my grandsire Pittheus' domain,
And which with one voice gives its throne to me,
I make you free as I; indeed, more free.

ARICIA

Your goodness stuns me, Sir. By this excess
Of noble sympathy for my distress,
You leave me, more than you could dream, still yoked

36

By those strict laws which you have just revoked.

HIPPOLYTUS

Athens, unsure of who should rule, divides
'Twixt you and me, and the Queen's son besides.

ARICIA

They speak of *me*?

HIPPOLYTUS

    Their laws, I'm well aware,
Would seem to void my claim as Theseus' heir,
Because an alien bore me. But if my one
Opponent were my brother, Phaedra's son,
I would, my lady, have the better cause,
And would contest those smug and foolish laws.
What checks me is a truer claim, your own;
I yield, or, rather, give you back, a throne
And scepter which your sires inherited
From that great mortal whom the Earth once bred.
Aegeus, though adopted, took their crown.
Theseus, his son, enlarged the state, cast down
Her foes, and was the choice of everyone,
Leaving your brothers in oblivion.
Now Athens calls you back within her walls.
Too long she's grieved for these dynastic brawls;
Too long your kinsmen's blood has drenched her earth,
Rising in steam from fields which gave it birth.
Troezen is mine, then. The domain of Crete
Offers to Phaedra's son a rich retreat.
Athens is yours. I go now to combine
In your cause all your partisans and mine.

37

ARICIA

These words so daze me that I almost fear
Some dream, some fancy has deceived my ear.
Am I awake? This plan which you have wrought—
What god, what god inspired you with the thought?
How just that, everywhere, men praise your name!
And how the truth, my lord, exceeds your fame!
You'll press my claims, against your interest?
'Twas kind enough that you should not detest
My house and me, should not be governed by
Old hatreds. . . .

HIPPOLYTUS

Hate you, Princess? No, not I.
I'm counted rough and proud, but don't assume
That I'm the issue of some monster's womb.
What hate-filled heart, what brute however wild
Could look upon your face and not grow mild?
Could I withstand your sweet, beguiling spell?

ARICIA

What's this, my lord?

HIPPOLYTUS

I've said too much. Ah, well,
My reason can't rein in my heart, I see.
Since I have spoken thus impetuously,
I must go on, my lady, and make plain
A secret I no longer can contain.
You see before you a most sorry prince,
A signal case of blind conceit. I wince
To think how I, Love's enemy, long disdained

Its bonds, and all whom passion had enchained;
How, pitying poor storm-tossed fools, I swore
Ever to view such tempests from the shore;
And now, like common men, for all my pride,
Am lost to reason in a raging tide.
One moment saw my vain defenses fall:
My haughty spirit is at last in thrall.
For six months now, ashamed and in despair,
I've borne Love's piercing arrow everywhere;
I've striven with you, and with myself, and though
I shun you, you are everywhere I go;
In the deep woods, your image haunts my sight;
The light of day, the shadows of the night,
All things call up your charms before my eyes
And vie to make my rebel heart your prize.
What use to struggle? I am not as before:
I seek myself, and find myself no more.
My bow, my javelins and my chariot pall;
What Neptune taught me once, I can't recall;
My idle steeds forget the voice they've known,
And the woods echo to my plaints alone.
You blush, perhaps, for so uncouth a love
As you have caused, and which I tell you of.
What a rude offer of my heart I make!
How strange a captive does your beauty take!
Yet that should make my offering seem more rich.
Remember, it's an unknown tongue in which
I speak; don't scorn these words, so poorly turned,
Which, but for you, my lips had never learned.

SCENE THREE

HIPPOLYTUS, ARICIA, THERAMENES, ISMENE

THERAMENES

My lord: the Queen, they tell me, comes this way.
It's you she seeks.

HIPPOLYTUS

Me?

THERAMENES

Why, I cannot say.
But Phaedra's sent ahead to let you know
That she must speak with you before you go.

HIPPOLYTUS

I, talk with Phaedra? What should we talk about?

ARICIA

My lord, you can't refuse to hear her out.
Malignant toward you as the Queen appears,
You owe some pity to her widow's tears.

40

HIPPOLYTUS

But now you'll leave me! And I shall sail before
I learn my fate from her whom I adore,
And in whose hands I leave this heart of mine. . . .

ARICIA

Go, Prince; pursue your generous design.
Make Athens subject to my royal sway.
All of your gifts I gladly take this day,
But that great empire, glorious though it be,
Is not the offering most dear to me.

SCENE FOUR

HIPPOLYTUS, THERAMENES

HIPPOLYTUS

Are we ready, friend? But the Queen's coming: hark.
Go, bid them trim our vessel; we soon embark.
Quick, give the order and return, that you
May free me from a vexing interview.

SCENE FIVE

PHAEDRA, HIPPOLYTUS, OENONE

PHAEDRA (*to Oenone, at stage rear*)

He's here. Blood rushes to my heart: I'm weak,
And can't recall the words I meant to speak.

OENONE

Think of your son, whose one hope rests with you.

PHAEDRA

My lord, they say you leave us. Before you do,
I've come to join your sorrows and my tears,
And tell you also of a mother's fears.
My son now lacks a father; and he will learn
Ere long that death has claimed me in my turn.
A thousand foes already seek to end
His hopes, which you, you only, can defend.
Yet I've a guilty fear that I have made
Your ears indifferent to his cries for aid.
I tremble lest you visit on my son
Your righteous wrath at what his mother's done.

HIPPOLYTUS

So base a thought I could not entertain.

43

PHAEDRA

Were you to hate me, I could not complain,
My lord. You've seen me bent on hurting you,
Though what was in my heart you never knew.
I sought your enmity. I would not stand
Your dwelling with me in the selfsame land.
I vilified you, and did not feel free
Till oceans separated you and me.
I went so far, indeed, as to proclaim
That none should, in my hearing, speak your name.
Yet if the crime prescribes the culprit's fate,
If I must hate you to have earned your hate,
Never did woman more deserve, my lord,
Your pity, or less deserve to be abhorred.

HIPPOLYTUS

It's common, Madam, that a mother spites
The stepson who might claim her children's rights.
I know that in a second marriage-bed
Anxiety and mistrust are often bred.
Another woman would have wished me ill
As you have, and perhaps been harsher still.

PHAEDRA

Ah, Prince! The Gods, by whom I swear it, saw
Fit to except me from that general law.
By what a different care am I beset!

HIPPOLYTUS

My lady, don't give way to anguish yet.
Your husband still may see the light of day;

44

Heaven may hear us, and guide his sail this way
Neptune protects him, and that deity
Will never fail to heed my father's plea.

PHAEDRA

No one goes twice among the dead; and since
Theseus has seen those gloomy regions, Prince,
No god will bring him back, hope though you may,
Nor greedy Acheron yield up his prey.
But no! He is not dead; he breathes in you.
My husband still seems present to my view.
I see him, speak with him. . . . Ah, my lord, I feel
Crazed with a passion which I can't conceal.

HIPPOLYTUS

In your strong love, what wondrous power lies!
Theseus, though dead, appears before your eyes.
For love of him your soul is still on fire.

PHAEDRA

Yes, Prince, I burn for him with starved desire,
Though not as he was seen among the shades,
The fickle worshiper of a thousand maids,
Intent on cuckolding the King of Hell;
But constant, proud, a little shy as well,
Young, charming, irresistible, much as we
Depict our Gods, or as you look to me.
He had your eyes, your voice, your virile grace,
It was your noble blush that tinged his face
When, crossing on the waves, he came to Crete
And made the hearts of Minos' daughters beat.
Where were you then? Why no Hippolytus

Among the flower of Greece he chose for us?
Why were you yet too young to join that band
Of heroes whom he brought to Minos' land?
You would have slain the Cretan monster then,
Despite the endless windings of his den.
My sister would have armed you with a skein
Of thread, to lead you from that dark domain.
But no: I'd first have thought of that design,
Inspired by love; the plan would have been mine.
It's I who would have helped you solve the maze,
My Prince, and taught you all its twisting ways.
What I'd have done to save that charming head!
My love would not have trusted to a thread.
No, Phaedra would have wished to share with you
Your perils, would have wished to lead you through
The Labyrinth, and thence have side by side
Returned with you; or else, with you, have died.

HIPPOLYTUS

Gods! What are you saying, Madam? Is Theseus not
Your husband, and my sire? Have you forgot?

PHAEDRA

You think that I forget those things? For shame,
My lord. Have I no care for my good name?

HIPPOLYTUS

Forgive me, Madam. I blush to have misread
The innocent intent of what you said.
I'm too abashed to face you; I shall take
My leave. . . .

46

PHAEDRA

Ah, cruel Prince, 'twas no mistake.
You understood; my words were all too plain.
Behold then Phaedra as she is, insane
With love for you. Don't think that I'm content
To be so, that I think it innocent,
Or that by weak compliance I have fed
The baneful love that clouds my heart and head.
Poor victim that I am of Heaven's curse,
I loathe myself; you could not hate me worse.
The Gods could tell how in this breast of mine
They lit the flame that's tortured all my line,
Those cruel Gods for whom it is but play
To lead a feeble woman's heart astray.
You too could bear me out; remember, do,
How I not only shunned but banished you.
I wanted to be odious in your sight;
To balk my love, I sought to earn your spite.
But what was gained by all of that distress?
You hated me the more; I loved no less,
And what you suffered made you still more dear.
I pined, I withered, scorched by many a tear.
That what I say is true, your eyes could see
If for a moment they could look at me.
What have I said? Do you suppose I came
To tell, of my free will, this tale of shame?
No, anxious for a son I dared not fail,
I came to beg you not to hate him. Frail
Indeed the heart is that's consumed by love!
Alas, it's only you I've spoken of.
Avenge yourself, now; punish my foul desire.
Come, rid the world, like your heroic sire,
Of one more monster; do as he'd have done.
Shall Theseus' widow dare to love his son?

47

No, such a monster is too vile to spare.
Here is my heart. Your blade must pierce me there.
In haste to expiate its wicked lust,
My heart already leaps to meet your thrust.
Strike, then. Or if your hatred and disdain
Refuse me such a blow, so sweet a pain,
If you'll not stain your hand with my abhorred
And tainted blood, lend me at least your sword.
Give it to me!

OENONE

        Just Gods! What's this, my Queen?
Someone is coming. You must not be seen.
Quick! Flee! You'll be disgraced if you delay.

SCENE SIX

THERAMENES

Did I see Phaedra vanish, dragged away?
Why do I find you pale and overcome?
Where is your sword, Sir? Why are you stricken dumb?

HIPPOLYTUS

Theramenes, I'm staggered. Let's go in haste.
I view myself with horror and distaste.
Phaedra . . . but no, great Gods! This thing must not
Be told, but ever buried and forgot.

THERAMENES

Sir, if you wish to sail, our ship's prepared.
But Athens' choice already is declared.
Her clans have all conferred; their leaders name
Your brother; Phaedra has achieved her aim.

HIPPOLYTUS

Phaedra?

THERAMENES

A herald's come at their command
To give the reins of state into her hand.
Her son is king.

HIPPOLYTUS

Gods, what she is you know;
Is it her virtue you've rewarded so?

THERAMENES

Meanwhile, it's rumored that the King's not dead,
That in Epirus he has shown his head.
But I, who searched that land, know well, my lord . . .

HIPPOLYTUS

No, let all clues be weighed, and none ignored.
We'll track this rumor down. Should it appear
Too insubstantial to detain us here,
We'll sail, and at whatever cost obtain
Great Athens' crown for one who's fit to reign.

ACT III

SCENE ONE

PHAEDRA, OENONE

PHAEDRA

Ah, let their honors deck some other brow.
Why urge me? How can I let them see me now?
D'you think to soothe my anguished heart with such
Vain solace? Hide me, rather. I've said too much.
My frenzied love's burst forth in act and word.
I've spoken what should never have been heard.
And how he heard me! How, with many a shift,
The brute pretended not to catch my drift!
How ardently he longed to turn and go!
And how his blushes caused my shame to grow!
Why did you come between my death and me?
Ah, when his sword-point neared my breast, did he
Turn pale with horror, and snatch back the blade?
No. I had touched it, and that touch had made
Him see it as a thing defiled and stained,
By which his pure hand must not be profaned.

OENONE

Dwelling like this on all you're grieved about,
You feed a flame which best were beaten out.
Would it not suit King Minos' child to find
In loftier concerns her peace of mind,

To flee an ingrate whom you love in vain,
Assume the conduct of the State, and reign?

PHAEDRA

I, reign? You'd trust the State to my control,
When reason rules no longer in my soul?
When passion's overthrown me? When, from the weight
Of shame I bear, I almost suffocate?
When I am dying?

OENONE

Flee him.

PHAEDRA

How could I? How?

OENONE

You once could banish him; can't you shun him now?

PHAEDRA

Too late. He knows what frenzy burns in me.
I've gone beyond the bounds of modesty.
My conqueror has heard my shame confessed,
And hope, despite me, has crept into my breast.
'Twas you who, when my life was near eclipse
And my last breath was fluttering on my lips,
Revived me with sweet lies that took me in
You said that now my love was free of sin.

54

OENONE

Ah, whether or not your woes are on my head,
To save you, what would I not have done or said?
But if an insult ever roused your spleen,
How can you pardon his disdainful mien?
How stonily, and with what cold conceit
He saw you all but grovel at his feet!
Oh, but his arrogance was rude and raw!
Why did not Phaedra see the man I saw?

PHAEDRA

This arrogance which irks you may grow less.
Bred in the forests, he has their ruggedness,
And, trained in harsh pursuits since he was young,
Has never heard, till now, love's gentle tongue.
No doubt it was surprise which made him mute,
And we do wrong to take him for a brute.

OENONE

Remember that an Amazon gave him life.

PHAEDRA

True: yet she learned to love like any wife.

OENONE

He has a savage hate for womankind.

PHAEDRA

No fear of rivals, then, need plague my mind.
Enough. Your counsels now are out of season.

Oenone, serve my madness, not my reason.
His heart is armored against love; let's seek
Some point where his defenses may be weak.
Imperial rule was in his thoughts, I feel;
He wanted Athens; that he could not conceal;
His vessels' prows already pointed there,
With sails all set and flapping in the air.
Go in my name, then; find this ambitious boy;
Dangle the crown before him like a toy.
His be the sacred diadem; in its stead
I ask no honor but to crown his head,
And yield a power I cannot hold. He'll school
My son in princely arts, teach him to rule,
And play for him, perhaps, a father's role.
Both mother and son I yield to his control.
Sway him, Oenone, by every wile that's known:
Your words will please him better than my own.
Sigh, groan, harangue him; picture me as dying;
Make use of supplication and of crying;
I'll sanction all you say. Go. I shall find,
When you return, what fate I am assigned.

SCENE TWO

PHAEDRA, *alone.*

O you who see to what I have descended,
Implacable Venus, is your vengeance ended?
Your shafts have all struck home; your victory's
Complete; what need for further cruelties?
If you would prove your pitiless force anew,
Attack a foe who's more averse to you.
Hippolytus flouts you; braving your divine
Wrath, he has never knelt before your shrine.
His proud ears seem offended by your name.
Take vengeance, Goddess; our causes are the same.
Force him to love . . . Oenone! You've returned
So soon? He hates me, then; your words were spurned.

SCENE THREE

OENONE

Madam, your hopeless love must be suppressed.
Call back the virtue which you once possessed.
The King, whom all thought dead, will soon be here,
Theseus has landed; Theseus is drawing near.
His people rush to see him, rapturous.
I'd just gone out to seek Hippolytus
When a great cry went up on every hand. .

PHAEDRA

My husband lives, Oenone; I understand.
I have confessed a love he will abhor.
He lives, and I have wronged him. Say no more

OENONE

What?

PHAEDRA

I foresaw this, but you changed my course
Your tears won out over my just remorse.

58

I might have died this morning, mourned and chaste;
I took your counsels, and I die disgraced.

OENONE

You die?

PHAEDRA

Just Heaven! Think what I have done!
My husband's coming; with him will be his son
I'll see the witness of my vile desire
Watch with what countenance I can greet his sire,
My heart still heavy with rejected sighs,
And tears which could not move him in my eyes.
Mindful of Theseus' honor, will he conceal
The scandal of my passion, do you feel,
Deceiving both his sire and king? Will he
Contain the horror that he feels for me?
His silence would be vain. What ill I've done
I know, Oenone, and I am not one
Of those bold women who, at ease in crime,
Are never seen to blush at any time.
I know my mad deeds, I recall them all.
I think that in this place each vault, each wall
Can speak, and that, impatient to accuse,
They wait to give my trusting spouse their news.
I'll die, then; from these horrors I'll be free.
Is it so sad a thing to cease to be?
Death is not fearful to a suffering mind
My only fear's the name I leave behind.
For my poor children, what a dire bequest!
Each has the blood of Jove within his breast,
But whatsoever pride of blood they share,
A mother's crime's a heavy thing to bear.

I tremble lest—alas, too truly!—they
Be chided for their mother's guilt some day.
I tremble lest, befouled by such a stain,
Neither should dare to lift his head again.

OENONE

I pity both of them; you could not be
More justified in your anxiety.
But why expose them to such insult? Why
Witness against yourself? You've but to die,
And folk will say that Phaedra, having strayed
From virtue, flees the husband she betrayed.
Hippolytus will rejoice that, cutting short
Your days, you lend his charges your support
How shall I answer your accuser? He
Will have no trouble in refuting me.
I'll watch him gloating hatefully, and hear
Him pour your shame in every listening ear
Let Heaven's fire consume me ere I do!
But come, speak frankly; is he still dear to you?
How do you see this prince so full of pride?

PHAEDRA

I see a monster, of whom I'm terrified.

OENONE

Then why should he triumph, when all can be reversed?
You fear the man. Dare to accuse him first
Of that which he might charge you with today.
What could belie you? The facts all point his way:
The sword which by good chance he left behind,
Your past mistrust, your present anguished mind,

His sire long cautioned by your warning voice,
And he sent into exile by your choice.

PHAEDRA

I, charge an innocent man with doing ill?

OENONE

Trust to my zeal. You've only to be still.
Like you I tremble, and feel a sharp regret.
I'd sooner face a thousand deaths. And yet
Since, lacking this sad remedy, you'll perish;
Since, above all, it is your life I cherish,
I'll speak to Theseus. He will do no more
Than doom his son to exile, as before.
A sire, when he must punish, is still a sire;
A lenient sentence will appease his ire.
But even if guiltless blood must flow, the cost
Were less than if your honor should be lost.
That honor is too dear to risk; its cause
Is priceless, and its dictates are your laws.
You must give up, since honor is at stake,
Everything, even virtue, for its sake.
Ah! Here comes Theseus.

PHAEDRA

               And Hippolytus, he
In whose cold eyes I read the end of me.
Do what you will; I yield myself to you.
In my confusion, I know not what to do.

SCENE FOUR

THESEUS, HIPPOLYTUS, PHAEDRA, OENONE, THERAMENES

THESEUS

Fortune has blessed me after long delay,
And in your arms, my lady . . .

PHAEDRA

                  Theseus, stay,
And don't profane the love those words express.
I am not worthy of your tenderness.
You have been wronged. Fortune or bitter fate
Did not, while you were absent, spare your mate.
Unfit to please you, or to be at your side,
Henceforth my only thought must be to hide.

SCENE FIVE

THESEUS

Why am I welcomed in this curious vein?

HIPPOLYTUS

That, Father, only Phaedra can explain.
But if my prayers can move you, grant me, Sir,
Never again to set my eyes on her.
Allow Hippolytus to say farewell
To any region where your wife may dwell.

THESEUS

Then you, my son, would leave me?

HIPPOLYTUS

                I never sought her:
When to this land she came, 'twas you who brought her.
Yes, you, my lord, when last you left us, bore
Aricia and the Queen to Troezen's shore.
You bade me be their guardian then; but how
Should any duties here detain me now?
Too long my youthful skill's been thrown away
Amidst these woods, upon ignoble prey.

63

May I not flee my idle pastimes here
To stain with worthier blood my sword or spear?
Before you'd lived as long as I have done,
More than one tyrant, monsters more than one
Had felt your strength of arm, your sword's keen blade;
Already, scourging such as sack and raid,
You had made safe the coasts of either sea.
The traveler lost his fears of banditry,
And Hercules, to whom your fame was known,
Welcomed your toils, and rested from his own.
But I, the unknown son of such a sire,
Lack even the fame my mother's deeds inspire.
Let me at long last show my courage, and,
If any monster has escaped your hand,
Bring back its pelt and lay it at your feet,
Or let me by a glorious death complete
A life that will defy oblivion
And prove to all the world I was your son.

THESEUS

What have I found? What horror fills this place,
And makes my family flee before my face?
If my unwished return makes all grow pale,
Why, Heaven, did you free me from my jail?
I'd one dear friend. He had a hankering
To steal the consort of Epirus' king.
I joined his amorous plot, though somewhat loath;
But outraged Fate brought blindness on us both.
The tyrant caught me, unarmed and by surprise.
I saw Pirithoüs with my weeping eyes
Flung by the barbarous king to monsters then,
Fierce beasts who drink the blood of luckless men.
Me he confined where never light invades,
In caverns near the empire of the shades.
After six months, Heaven pitied my mischance.

Escaping from my guardians' vigilance,
I cleansed the world of one more fiend, and threw
To his own beasts his bloody corpse to chew.
But now when, joyful, I return to see
The dearest whom the Gods have left to me;
Now, when my spirits, glad once more and light,
Would feast again upon that cherished sight,
I'm met with shudders and with frightened faces;
All flee me, all deny me their embraces.
Touched by the very terror I beget,
I wish I were Epirus' prisoner yet.
Speak! Phaedra says that I've been wronged. By whom?
Why has the culprit not yet met his doom?
Has Greece, so often sheltered by my arm,
Chosen to shield this criminal from harm?
You're silent. Is my own son, if you please,
In some alliance with my enemies?
I shall go in, and end this maddening doubt.
Both crime and culprit must be rooted out,
And Phaedra tell why she is so distraught.

SCENE SIX

HIPPOLYTUS

How her words chilled me! What was in her thought?
Will Phaedra, who is still her frenzy's prey,
Accuse herself, and throw her life away?
What will the King say? Gods! What love has done
To poison all this house while he was gone!
And I, who burn for one who bears his curse,
Am altered in his sight, and for the worse!
I've dark forebodings; something ill draws near.
Yet surely innocence need never fear.
Come, let's consider now how I may best
Revive the kindness in my father's breast,
And tell him of a love which he may take
Amiss, but all his power cannot shake.

ACT IV

SCENE ONE

THESEUS

What do I hear? How bold and treacherous
To plot against his father's honor thus!
How sternly you pursue me, Destiny!
Where shall I turn? I know not. Where can I be?
O love and kindness not repaid in kind!
Outrageous scheme of a degenerate mind!
To seek his lustful end he had recourse,
Like any blackguard, to the use of force.
I recognize the sword his passion drew—
My gift, bestowed with nobler deeds in view.
Why did our ties of blood prove no restraint?
Why too did Phaedra make no prompt complaint?
Was it to spare the culprit?

OENONE

     It was rather
That she, in pity, wished to spare his father.
Ashamed because her beauty had begot
So foul a passion, and so fierce a plot,
By her own hand, my lord, she sought to die,
And darken thus the pure light of her eye.
I saw her raise her arm; to me you owe
Her life, because I ran and stayed the blow.

69

Now, pitying both her torment and your fears,
I have, against my will, spelled out her tears.

THESEUS

The traitor! Ah, no wonder he turned pale.
When first he sighted me, I saw him quail.
'Twas strange to see no greeting in his face.
My heart was frozen by his cold embrace.
But did he, even in Athens, manifest
This guilty love by which he is possessed?

OENONE

The Queen, remember, could not tolerate him.
It was his infamous love which made her hate him.

THESEUS

That love, I take it, was rekindled here
In Troezen?

OENONE

I've told you all, my lord. I fear
I've left the Queen too long in mortal grief.
Let me now haste to bring her some relief.

SCENE TWO

THESEUS, HIPPOLYTUS

THESEUS

Ah, here he comes. Gods! By that noble mien
What eye would not be duped, as mine has been!
Why must the brow of an adulterer
Be stamped with virtue's sacred character?
Should there not be clear signs by which one can
Divine the heart of a perfidious man?

HIPPOLYTUS

May I enquire what louring cloud obscures,
My lord, that royal countenance of yours?
Dare you entrust the secret to your son?

THESEUS

Dare you appear before me, treacherous one?
Monster, at whom Jove's thunder should be hurled!
Foul brigand, like those of whom I cleansed the world!
Now that your vile, unnatural love has led
You even to attempt your father's bed,
How dare you show your hated self to me
Here in the precincts of your infamy,

71

Rather than seek some unknown land where fame
Has never brought the tidings of my name?
Fly, wretch. Don't brave the hate which fills my soul,
Or tempt a wrath it pains me to control.
I've earned, forevermore, enough disgrace
By fathering one who'd do a deed so base,
Without your death upon my hands, to soil
A noble history of heroic toil.
Fly, and unless you wish to join the band
Of knaves who've met quick justice at my hand,
Take care lest by the sun's eye you be found
Setting an insolent foot upon this ground.
Now, never to return, be off; take flight;
Cleanse all my realms of your abhorrent sight.
And you, O Neptune, if by courage I
Once cleared your shores of murderers, hear my cry.
Recall that, as reward for that great task,
You swore to grant the first thing I should ask.
Pent in a cruel jail for endless hours,
I never called on your immortal powers.
I've hoarded up the aid you promised me
Till greater need should justify my plea.
I make it now. Avenge a father's wrong.
Seize on this traitor, and let your rage be strong.
Drown in his blood his brazen lust. I'll know
Your favor by the fury that you show.

HIPPOLYTUS

Phaedra accuses me of lust? I'm weak
With horror at the thought, and cannot speak;
By all these sudden blows I'm overcome;
They leave me stupefied, and stricken dumb.

72

THESEUS

Scoundrel, you thought that Phaedra'd be afraid
To tell of the depraved assault you made.
You should have wrested from her hands the hilt
Of the sharp sword that points now to your guilt;
Or, better, crowned your outrage of my wife
By robbing her at once of speech and life.

HIPPOLYTUS

In just resentment of so black a lie,
I might well let the truth be known, but I
Suppress what comes too near your heart. Approve,
My lord, a silence which bespeaks my love.
Restrain, as well, your mounting rage and woe:
Review my life; recall the son you know.
Great crimes grow out of small ones. If today
A man first oversteps the bounds, he may
Abuse in time all laws and sanctities;
For crime, like virtue, ripens by degrees;
But when has one seen innocence, in a trice,
So change as to embrace the ways of vice?
Not in a single day could time transmute
A virtuous man to an incestuous brute.
I had an Amazon mother, brave and chaste,
Whose noble blood my life has not debased.
And when I left her hands, 'twas Pittheus, thought
Earth's wisest man, by whom my youth was taught.
I shall not vaunt such merits as I've got,
But if one virtue's fallen to my lot,
It is, my lord, a fierce antipathy
To just that vice imputed now to me.
It is for that Hippolytus is known

In Greece—for virtue cold and hard as stone.
By harsh austerity I am set apart.
The daylight is not purer than my heart.
Yet I, it's charged, consumed by lechery . . .

THESEUS

This very boast betrays your guilt. I see
What all your vaunted coldness signifies:
Phaedra alone could please your lustful eyes;
No other woman moved you, or could inspire
Your scornful heart with innocent desire.

HIPPOLYTUS

No, Father: hear what it's time I told you of;
I have not scorned to feel a blameless love.
I here confess my only true misdeed:
I am in love, despite what you decreed.
Aricia has enslaved me; my heart is won,
And Pallas' daughter has subdued your son.
I worship her against your orders, Sir,
Nor could I burn or sigh except for her.

THESEUS

You love her? Gods! But no, I see your game.
You play the criminal to clear your name.

HIPPOLYTUS

Six months I've shunned her whom my heart adored.
I came in fear to tell you this, my lord.
Why must you be so stubbornly mistaken?
To win your trust, what great oath must be taken?
By Earth, and Heaven, and all the things that be . . .

[*Act Four* · *Scene Two*]

THESEUS

A rascal never shrinks from perjury.
Cease now to weary me with sly discourse,
If your false virtue has but that resource.

HIPPOLYTUS

My virtue may seem false and sly to you,
But Phaedra has good cause to know it true.

THESEUS

Ah, how your impudence makes my temper boil!

HIPPOLYTUS

How long shall I be banished? On what soil?

THESEUS

Were you beyond Alcides' pillars, I
Would think yet that a rogue was too nearby.

HIPPOLYTUS

Who will befriend me now—a man suspected
Of such a crime, by such a sire rejected?

THESEUS

Go look for friends who think adultery cause
For accolades, and incest for applause,
Yes, ingrates, traitors, to law and honor blind,
Fit to protect a blackguard of your kind.

75

HIPPOLYTUS

Incest! Adultery! Are these still your themes?
I'll say no more. Yet Phaedra's mother, it seems,
And, as you know, Sir, all of Phaedra's line
Knew more about such horrors than did mine.

THESEUS

So! You dare storm and rage before my face?
I tell you for the last time: leave this place.
Be off, before I'm roused to violence
And have you, in dishonor, driven hence.

SCENE THREE

THESEUS, *alone.*

Poor wretch, the path you take will end in blood.
What Neptune swore by Styx, that darkest flood
Which frights the Gods themselves, he'll surely do.
And none escapes when vengeful Gods pursue.
I loved you; and in spite of what you've done,
I mourn your coming agonies, my son.
But you have all too well deserved my curse.
When was a father ever outraged worse?
Just Gods, who see this grief which drives me wild,
How could I father such a wicked child?

SCENE FOUR

PHAEDRA, THESEUS

PHAEDRA

My lord, I hasten to you, full of dread.
I heard your threatening voice, and what it said.
Pray Heaven no deed has followed on your threat.
I beg you, if there is time to save him yet,
To spare your son; spare me the dreadful sound
Of blood, your own blood, crying from the ground.
Do not impose on me the endless woe
Of having caused your hand to make it flow.

THESEUS

No, Madam, my blood's not on my hands. But he,
The thankless knave, has not escaped from me.
A God's great hand will be his nemesis
And your avenger. Neptune owes me this.

PHAEDRA

Neptune! And will your angry prayers be heard?

THESEUS

What! Are you fearful lest he keep his word?
No, rather join me in my righteous pleas.

Recount to me my son's black treacheries;
Stir up my sluggish wrath, that's still too cold.
He has done crimes of which you've not been told:
Enraged at you, he slanders your good name:
Your mouth is full of lies, he dares to claim;
He states that, heart and soul, his love is pledged
To Aricia.

PHAEDRA

What, my lord!

THESEUS

　　　　　So he alleged;
But I saw through so obvious a trick.
Let's hope that Neptune's justice will be quick.
I go now to his altars, to implore
A prompt fulfillment of the oath he swore.

SCENE FIVE

PHAEDRA, *alone.*

He's gone. What news assails my ear? What ill-
Extinguished fire flares in my bosom still?
By what a thunderbolt I am undone!
I'd flown here with one thought, to save his son.
Escaping from Oenone's arms by force,
I'd yielded to my torturing remorse.
How far I might have gone, I cannot guess.
Guilt might perhaps have driven me to confess.
Perhaps, had shock not caused my voice to fail,
I might have blurted out my hideous tale.
Hippolytus can feel, but not for me!
Aricia has his love, his loyalty!
Gods! When he steeled himself against my sighs
With that forbidding brow, those scornful eyes,
I thought his heart, which love-darts could not strike,
Was armed against all womankind alike.
And yet another's made his pride surrender;
Another's made his cruel eyes grow tender.
Perhaps his heart is easy to ensnare.
It's me, alone of women, he cannot bear!
Shall I defend a man by whom I'm spurned?

SCENE SIX

PHAEDRA, OENONE

PHAEDRA

Oenone dear, do you know what I have learned?

OENONE

No, but in truth I'm quaking still with fear
Of the wild urge that sent you rushing here:
I feared some blunder fatally adverse.

PHAEDRA

I had a rival. Who would have thought it, Nurse?

OENONE

What?

PHAEDRA

    Yes, Hippolytus is in love; it's true.
That savage creature no one could subdue,
Who scorned regard, who heard no lovers' pleas,
That tiger whom I viewed with trembling knees,
Is tame now, broken by a woman's art:
Aricia's found the way into his heart.

OENONE

Aricia?

PHAEDRA

O pain I never felt before!
What new, sharp torments have I kept in store!
All that I've suffered—frenzies, fears, the dire
Oppression of remorse, my heart on fire,
The merciless rebuff he gave to me—
All were but foretastes of this agony.
They love each other! By what magic, then,
Did they beguile me? Where did they meet, and when?
You knew. Why did you keep me unaware,
Deceived as to their furtive love-affair?
Were they much seen together? Were they known
To haunt the deep woods, so as to be alone?
Alas, they'd perfect liberty to meet.
Heaven smiled on hearts so innocent and sweet;
Without remorse, they savored love's delight;
For them, each dawn arose serene and bright—
While I, creation's outcast, hid away
From the Sun's eye, and fled the light of day.
Death was the only God I dared implore.
I longed for him; I prayed to be no more.
Quenching my thirst with tears, and fed on gall,
Yet in my woe too closely watched by all,
I dared not weep and grieve in fullest measure;
I sipped in secret at that bitter pleasure;
And often, wearing a serene disguise,
I kept my pain from welling in my eyes.

OENONE

What will their love avail them? They will never
Meet again.

PHAEDRA

But they will love forever.
Even as I speak—ah, deadly thought!—they dare
To mock my crazed desire and my despair.
Despite this exile which will make them part,
They swear forever to be joined in heart.
No, no, their bliss I cannot tolerate,
Oenone. Take pity on my jealous hate.
Aricia must die. Her odious house
Must once more feel the anger of my spouse.
Nor can the penalty be light, for her
Misdeeds are darker than her brothers' were.
In my wild jealousy I will plead with him.
I'll what? Has my poor reason grown so dim?
I, jealous! And it's with Theseus I would plead!
My husband lives, and still my passions feed
On whom? Toward whom do all my wishes tend?
At every word, my hair stands up on end.
The measure of my crimes is now replete.
I foul the air with incest and deceit.
My murderous hands are itching to be stained
With innocent blood, that vengeance be obtained.
Wretch that I am, how can I live, how face
The sacred Sun, great elder of my race?
My grandsire was, of all the Gods, most high;
My forebears fill the world, and all the sky.
Where can I hide? For Hades' night I yearn.
No, there my father holds the dreadful urn
Entrusted to his hands by Fate, it's said:
There Minos judges all the ashen dead.
Ah, how his shade will tremble with surprise
To see his daughter brought before his eyes—
Forced to confess a throng of sins, to tell
Of crimes perhaps unheard of yet in Hell!
What will you say then, Father? As in a dream,

83

I see you drop the fearful urn; you seem
To ponder some new torment fit for her,
Yourself become your own child's torturer.
Forgive me. A cruel God destroys your line;
Behold her hand in these mad deeds of mine.
My heart, alas! not once enjoyed the fruit
Of its dark, shameful crime. In fierce pursuit,
Misfortune dogs me till, with my last breath,
My sad life shall, in torments, yield to death.

OENONE

My lady, don't give in to needless terror.
Look freshly at your pardonable error.
You love. But who can conquer Destiny?
Lured by a fatal spell, you were not free.
Is that a marvel hitherto unknown?
Has Love entrapped no heart but yours alone?
Weakness is natural to us, is it not?
You are a mortal; accept your mortal lot.
To chafe against our frail estate is vain.
Even the Gods who on Olympus reign,
And with their thunders chasten men for crime,
Have felt illicit passions many a time.

PHAEDRA

Ah, what corrupting counsels do I hear?
Wretch! Will you pour such poison in my ear
Right to the end? Look how you've ruined me.
You dragged me back to all I sought to flee.
You blinded me to duty; called it no wrong
To see Hippolytus, whom I'd shunned so long.
Ah, meddling creature, why did your sinful tongue
Falsely accuse a soul so pure and young?
He'll die, it may be, if the Gods can bear

84

To grant his maddened father's impious prayer.
No, say no more. Go, monster whom I hate.
Go, let me face at last my own sad fate.
May Heaven reward you for your deeds! And may
Your punishment forever give dismay
To all who, like yourself, by servile arts
Nourish the weaknesses of princes' hearts,
Incline them to pursue the baser path,
And smooth for them the way to sin and wrath—
Accursèd flatterers, the worst of things
That Heaven's anger can bestow on kings!

OENONE

I've given my life to her. Ah, Gods! It hurts
To be thus thanked. Yet I have my just deserts.

SCENE ONE

ARICIA

Come, in this mortal danger, will you not make
Your loving sire aware of his mistake?
If, scorning all my tears, you can consent
To parting and an endless banishment,
Go, leave Aricia in her life alone.
But first assure the safety of your own.
Defend your honor against a foul attack,
And force your sire to call his prayers back.
There yet is time. What moves you, if you please,
Not to contest Queen Phaedra's calumnies?
Tell Theseus the truth.

HIPPOLYTUS

     What more should I
Have told him? How she smirched their marriage-tie?
How could I, by disclosing everything,
Humiliate my father and my king?
It's you alone I've told these horrors to.
I've bared my heart but to the Gods and you.
Judge of my love, which forced me to confide
What even from myself I wished to hide.
But, mind you, keep this secret ever sealed.
Forget, if possible, all that I've revealed,

And never let those pure lips part to bear
Witness, my lady, to this vile affair.
Let us rely upon the Gods' high laws:
Their honor binds them to defend my cause;
And Phaedra, sooner or later brought to book,
Will blush for crimes their justice cannot brook.
To that restraint I ask you to agree.
In all things else, just anger makes me free.
Come, break away from this, your slavish plight;
Dare follow me, dare join me in my flight;
Be quit of an accursèd country where
Virtue must breathe a foul and poisoned air.
Under the cover of this turbulence
Which my disfavor brings, slip quickly hence.
I can assure a safe escape for you.
Your only guards are of my retinue.
Strong states will champion us; upon our side
Is Sparta; Argos' arms are open wide:
Let's plead then to these friends our righteous case,
Lest Phaedra, profiting by our disgrace,
Deny our lineal claims to either throne,
And pledge her son my birthright and your own.
Come, let us seize the moment; we mustn't wait.
What holds you back? You seem to hesitate.
It's zeal for you that moves me to be bold.
When I am all on fire, what makes you cold?
Are you afraid to join a banished man?

ARICIA

Alas, my lord, how sweet to share that ban!
What deep delight, as partner of your lot,
To live with you, by all the world forgot!
But since no blessèd tie unites us two,
Can I, in honor, flee this land with you?
The sternest code, I know, would not deny

My right to break your father's bonds and fly;
I'd grieve no loving parents thus; I'm free,
As all are, to escape from tyranny.
But, Sir, you love me, and my fear of shame . . .

HIPPOLYTUS

Ah, never doubt my care for your good name.
It is a nobler plan that I propose:
Flee with your husband from our common foes.
Freed by mischance, since Heaven so commands,
We need no man's consent to join our hands.
Not every nuptial needs the torch's light.
At Troezen's gate, amidst that burial site
Where stand our princes' ancient sepulchers,
There is a temple feared by perjurers.
No man there dares to break his faith, on pain
Of instant doom, or swear an oath in vain;
There all deceivers, lest they surely die,
Bridle their tongues and are afraid to lie.
There, if you trust me, we will go, and of
Our own accord shall pledge eternal love;
The temple's God will witness to our oath;
We'll pray that he be father to us both.
I shall invoke all deities pure and just.
The chaste Diana, Juno the august,
And all the Gods who know my faithfulness
Will guarantee the vows I shall profess.

ARICIA

The King is coming. Go, Prince, make no delay.
To cloak my own departure, I'll briefly stay.
Go, go; but leave with me some faithful guide
Who'll lead my timid footsteps to your side.

SCENE TWO

THESEUS, ARICIA, ISMENE

THESEUS

O Gods, bring light into my troubled mind;
Show me the truth which I've come here to find.

ARICIA

Make ready for our flight, Ismene dear.

SCENE THREE

THESEUS, ARICIA

THESEUS

Your color changes, Madam, and you appear
Confused. Why was Hippolytus here with you?

ARICIA

He came, my lord, to say a last adieu.

THESEUS

Ah, yes. You've tamed his heart, which none could
    capture,
And taught his stubborn lips to sigh with rapture.

ARICIA

I shan't deny the truth, my lord. No, he
Did not inherit your malignity,
Nor treat me as a criminal, in your fashion.

THESEUS

I see. He's sworn, no doubt, eternal passion.
Put no reliance on the vows of such
A fickle lover. He's promised others as much.

ARICIA

He, Sir?

THESEUS

You should have taught him not to stray.
How could you share his love in that base way?

ARICIA

How could you let a shameful lie besmear
The stainless honor of his young career?
Have you so little knowledge of his heart?
Can't you tell sin and innocence apart?
Must some black cloud bedim your eyes alone
To the bright virtue for which your son is known?
Shall slander ruin him? That were too much to bear.
Turn back: repent now of your murderous prayer.
Fear, my lord, fear lest the stern deities
So hate you as to grant your wrathful pleas.
Our sacrifices anger Heaven at times;
Its gifts are often sent to scourge our crimes.

THESEUS

Your words can't cover up that sin of his:
Love's blinded you to what the scoundrel is.
But I've sure proofs on which I may rely:
I have seen tears—yes, tears which could not lie.

ARICIA

Take care, my lord. You have, in many lands,
Slain countless monsters with your conquering hands;
But all are not destroyed; there still lives one

Who . . . No, I am sworn to silence by your son.
Knowing his wish to shield your honor, I'd
Afflict him if I further testified.
I'll imitate his reticence, and flee
Your presence, lest the truth should burst from me.

SCENE FOUR

THESEUS, *alone.*

What does she mean? These speeches which begin
And then break off—what are they keeping in?
Is this some sham those two have figured out?
Have they conspired to torture me with doubt?
But I myself, despite my stern control—
What plaintive voice cries from my inmost soul?
I feel a secret pity, a surge of pain.
Oenone must be questioned once again.
I'll have more light on this. Not all is known.
Guards, go and bring Oenone here, alone.

SCENE FIVE

PANOPE

I don't know what the Queen may contemplate,
My lord, but she is in a frightening state.
Mortal despair is what her looks bespeak;
Death's pallor is already on her cheek.
Oenone, driven from her in disgrace,
Has thrown herself into the sea's embrace.
None knows what madness caused the thing she did;
Beneath the waves she lies forever hid.

THESEUS

What do you tell me?

PANOPE

          This death has left the Queen
No calmer; her distraction grows more keen.
At moments, to allay her dark unrest,
She clasps her children, weeping, to her breast;
Then, with a sudden horror, she will shove
Them both away, and starve her mother-love.
She wanders aimlessly about the floor;
Her blank eye does not know us any more.
Thrice she has written; and thrice, before she'd done,

Torn up the letter which she had begun.
We cannot help her. I beg you, Sire, to try.

THESEUS

Oenone's dead? And Phaedra wants to die?
O bring me back my son, and let him clear
His name! If he'll but speak, I now will hear.
O Neptune, let your gifts not be conferred
Too swiftly; let my prayers go unheard.
Too much I've trusted what may not be true,
Too quickly raised my cruel hands to you.
How I'd despair if what I asked were done!

SCENE SIX

THESEUS, THERAMENES

THESEUS

Is it you, Theramenes? Where have you left my son?
You've been his mentor since his tenderest years.
But why do I behold you drenched in tears?
Where's my dear son?

THERAMENES

                    Too late, Sire, you restore
Your love to him. Hippolytus is no more.

THESEUS

Gods!

THERAMENES

    I have seen the best of mortals slain,
My lord, and the least guilty, I maintain.

THESEUS

My son is dead? What! Just when I extend
My arms to him, Heaven's haste has caused his end?
What thunderbolt bereaved me? What was his fate?

THERAMENES

Scarcely had we emerged from Troezen's gate:
He drove his chariot, and his soldiery
Were ranged about him, mute and grave as he.
Brooding, he headed toward Mycenae. Lax
In his hands, the reins lay on his horses' backs.
His haughty chargers, quick once to obey
His voice, and give their noble spirits play,
Now, with hung head and mournful eye, seemed part
Of the sad thoughts that filled their master's heart.
Out of the sea-deeps then a frightful cry
Arose, to tear the quiet of the sky,
And a dread voice from far beneath the ground
Replies in groans to that appalling sound.
Our hearts congeal; blood freezes in our veins.
The horses, hearing, bristle up their manes.
And now there rises from the sea's calm breast
A liquid mountain with a seething crest.
The wave approaches, breaks, and spews before
Our eyes a raging monster on the shore.
His huge brow's armed with horns; the spray unveils
A body covered all with yellow scales;
Half bull he is, half dragon; fiery, bold;
His thrashing tail contorts in fold on fold.
With echoing bellows now he shakes the strand.
The sky, aghast, beholds him; he makes the land
Shudder; his foul breath chokes the atmosphere;
The wave which brought him in recoils in fear.
All flee, and in a nearby temple save
Their lives, since it is hopeless to be brave.
Hippolytus alone dares make a stand.
He checks his chargers, javelins in hand,
Has at the monster and, with a sure-aimed throw,
Pierces his flank: a great wound starts to flow.
In rage and pain the beast makes one dread spring,

Falls near the horses' feet, still bellowing,
Rolls over toward them, with fiery throat takes aim
And covers them with smoke and blood and flame.
Sheer panic takes them; deaf now, they pay no heed
To voice or curb, but bolt in full stampede;
Their master strives to hold them back, in vain.
A bloody slaver drips from bit and rein.
It's said that, in that tumult, some caught sight
Of a God who spurred those dusty flanks to flight.
Fear drives them over rocks; the axletree
Screeches and breaks. The intrepid Prince must see
His chariot dashed to bits, for all his pains;
He falls at last, entangled in the reins.
Forgive my grief. That cruel sight will be
An everlasting source of tears for me.
I've seen, my lord, the heroic son you bred
Dragged by the horses which his hand had fed.
His shouts to them but make their fear more strong.
His body seems but one great wound, ere long.
The plain re-echoes to our cries of woe.
At last, their headlong fury starts to slow:
They stop, then, near that graveyard which contains,
In royal tombs, his forebears' cold remains.
I run to him in tears; his guards are led
By the bright trail of noble blood he shed;
The rocks are red with it; the briars bear
Their red and dripping trophies of his hair.
I reach him; speak his name; his hand seeks mine;
His eyelids lift a moment, then decline.
"Heaven takes," he says, "my innocent life away.
Protect my sad Aricia, I pray.
If ever, friend, my sire is disabused,
And mourns his son who falsely was accused,
Bid him appease my blood and plaintive shade
By dealing gently with that captive maid.
Let him restore . . ." His voice then died away,

And in my arms a mangled body lay
Which the Gods' wrath had claimed, a sorry prize
Which even his father would not recognize.

THESEUS

My son, dear hope whom folly made me kill!
O ruthless Gods, too well you did my will!
I'll henceforth be the brokenest of men.

THERAMENES

Upon this scene came shy Aricia then,
Fleeing your wrath, and ready to espouse
Your son before the Gods by holy vows.
She comes, and sees the red and steaming grass;
She sees—no sight for loving eyes, alas!—
Hippolytus sprawled there, lacking form or hue.
At first, she won't believe her loss is true.
Not recognizing her beloved, she
Both looks at him and asks where he may be.
At last she knows too well what's lying there;
She lifts to the Gods a sad, accusing stare;
Then, moaning, cold, and all but dead, the sweet
Maid drops unconscious at her lover's feet.
Ismene, weeping, kneels and seeks to bring
Her back to life—a life of suffering.
And I, my lord, have come, who now detest
This world, to bring a hero's last request,
And so perform the bitter embassy
Which, with his dying breath, he asked of me.
But look: his mortal enemy comes this way.

SCENE SEVEN

THESEUS, PHAEDRA, THERAMENES, PANOPE, GUARDS

THESEUS

Well, Madam, my son's no more; you've won the day!
Ah, but what qualms I feel! What doubts torment
My heart, and plead that he was innocent!
But, Madam, claim your victim. He is dead.
Enjoy his death, unjust or merited.
I'm willing to be evermore deceived.
You've called him guilty; let it be believed.
His death is grief enough for me to bear
Without my further probing this affair,
Which could not bring his dear life back again,
And might perhaps but aggravate my pain.
No, far from you and Troezen, I shall flee
My dead son's torn and bloody memory.
It will pursue me ever, like a curse:
Would I were banished from the universe!
All seems to chide my wicked wrathfulness.
My very fame now adds to my distress.
How shall I hide, who have a name so great?
Even the Gods' high patronage I hate.
I go to mourn this murderous gift of theirs,
Nor trouble them again with useless prayers.
Do for me what they might, it could not pay
For what their deadly favor took away.

PHAEDRA

Theseus, my wrongful silence must be ended.
Your guiltless son must be at last defended.
He did no ill.

THESEUS

How curst a father am I!
I doomed him, trusting in your heartless lie!
Do you think to be excused for such a crime?

PHAEDRA

Hear me, my lord. I have but little time.
I was the lustful and incestuous one
Who dared desire your chaste and loyal son.
Heaven lit a fatal blaze within my breast.
Detestable Oenone did the rest.
She, fearing lest Hippolytus, who knew
Of my vile passion, might make it known to you,
Abused my weakness and, by a vicious ruse,
Made haste to be the first one to accuse.
For that she's paid; fleeing my wrath, she found
Too mild a death, and in the waves is drowned.
Much though I wished to die then by the sword,
Your son's pure name cried out to be restored.
That my remorse be told, I chose instead
A slower road that leads down to the dead.
I drank, to give my burning veins some peace,
A poison which Medea brought to Greece.
Already, to my heart, the venom gives
An alien coldness, so that it scarcely lives;
Already, to my sight, all clouds and fades—
The sky, my spouse, the world my life degrades;

Death dims my eyes, which soiled what they could see,
Restoring to the light its purity.

PANOPE

She's dead, my lord!

THESEUS

     Would that I could inter
The memory of her black misdeeds with her!
Let's go, since now my error's all too clear,
And mix my poor son's blood with many a tear,
Embrace his dear remains, and expiate
The fury of a prayer which now I hate.
To his great worth all honor shall be paid,
And, further to appease his angry shade,
Aricia, despite her brothers' offense,
Shall be my daughter from this moment hence.

Books by Richard Wilbur available
from Harcourt Brace & Company
in Harvest paperback editions

New and Collected Poems
The Poems of Richard Wilbur

TRANSLATIONS
Molière's *The Misanthrope* and *Tartuffe*
Molière's *The School for Husbands* and *Sganarelle*
Molière's *The School for Wives* and *The Learned Ladies*
Molière's *Tartuffe*
Racine's *Andromache*
Racine's *Phaedra*